They that hope in the Lord will renew their strength, they will soar as with eagles' wings; they will run and not grow weary, walk and not grow faint.

Isaiah 40:31

The intent and
purpose of this volume is to
give you faith, hope and inspiration.
Hopefully it will help bring peace and
tranquility into your life. May it be a
reminder of God's love, guidance
and His many blessings.

Our publications help to support our work
for needy children in over 130 countries
around the world. Through our programs,
thousands of children are fed, clothed,
educated, sheltered and given
the opportunity to live
decent lives.

Salesian Missions wishes to extend special thanks and gratitude to our generous poet friends and to the publishers who have given us permission to reprint material included in this book. Every effort has been made to give proper acknowledgments. Any omissions or errors are deeply regretted, and the publisher, upon notification, will be pleased to make the necessary corrections in subsequent editions.

Hope on the Horizon
from the Salesian Collection

Compiled and Edited by
Jennifer Grimaldi

Illustrated by
Russell Bushée, Paul Scully,
Frank Massa, Dorian Lee Remine,
Bob Pantelone, Terry Meider,
Gail Pepin, and Robert VanSteinburg

Contents

...listen from Your heavenly dwelling place, hear their prayer and petitions, and uphold their cause. Forgive Your people who have sinned against You.
2 Chronicles 6:39

Just a Prayer Away

Sometimes it seems, life hands us lemons,
When troubles come our way.
But if we petition our God of Love,
He will hear us when we pray.

"Ask, and it shall be given,"
The Holy Scriptures say.
If we ask with a contrite heart,
God can take our troubles away.

Help is just a prayer away,
A loving God is always there.
When tribulations overwhelm us…
The answer is – "Go to God in prayer."

Charles Clevenger

*You listen, Lord, to the needs of
the poor; You encourage them
and hear their prayers.*
Psalm 10:17

Cast Worry Aside

Trust in God our Creator
And cast your worries aside –
There isn't a need to fret and tremble,
For our Heavenly Father will provide.
He fashioned each decorative flower
So dainty in grace and in form,
Created the multicolorful rainbow
After a springtime shower and storm.
Every single hair on our head and wee fingerprints
Were numbered and designed by Him,
So just have faith that God is nearby
When your candle burns slow and dim.

Rolling mountains and deep valleys,
God simply spoke into place,
For nothing is impossible –
Remember, He saved us by grace!
So cast aside that web of worries
Unto God's throne and He'll show you the way,
To have peace of mind and a joyful life
By simply "trusting" in Him today.

Linda C. Grazulis

Words

Only a few words…
But how they can bless
A soul that's discouraged
And in deep distress.

How easy to choose
The word that can bring
New hope and courage
To cause hearts to sing.

Only a few words…
And yet they hold power
Of blessing or cursing
This very hour.

Will we choose words
Of discouragement or sadness?
Or will our words bring
Joy, comfort and gladness?

Helen Gleason

While Singing Songs of Laud

(A Shakespearean Sonnet)

With earnest thoughts, my mind is set on Thee,
My Savior, God, Who saved me from sin;
Deep in my heart there sings a melody
Of praises that repeats over again.
The love You shower o'er me every day
Fills up my soul and sets all sorrows free.
No greater gift could ever come my way
Than the sacrifice made at Calvary.
The love of God has healed my broken heart,
No more will I be orphaned and alone;
Forgiven, now, I've found a brand new start
And one day, I will kneel before His throne.
I'll lay my crown of life at Jesus's feet,
While singing songs of laud, so soft and sweet.

Nancy Watson Dodrill

Never Alone

When life seems it isn't worth living,
And burdens are too hard to bear,
Heartaches and trials surround you –
It seems there is no one to care.

In the midst of this grief and sorrow,
Look up to God on the throne:
He has promised never to leave you,
He will never forsake His own.

He will comfort when your heart is breaking,
He will answer when you feel so unknown,
He will be there whenever you seek Him,
And He never will leave you alone.

Frances Culp Wolfe

*God alone is my rock and
salvation, my secure height;
I shall never fall.*
Psalm 62:3

Life's Goal

If you want to reach your life-long goal,
Then you must have a plan.
It's like starting a fire with a few little chips
And you blow on the flame 'til it spreads like a fan.

The plan has many pages
Before the dream you can realize.
The steps must be followed in order
Or the dream will be no prize.

We all want to do things quickly
Before the setting of the sun.
Yet we need to strive with patience
If our work will be well-done.

When we follow the plan without skipping steps,
The result cannot be beat.
The goal can be met with God as Guide
To make your life complete.

M. Elaine Fowser

...I continue my pursuit toward
the goal, the prize of God's upward
calling, in Christ Jesus.
Philippians 3:14

Perseverance

There are times when we are weary
And burdened down with grief,
When our world caves in on us
And we can't find relief.
Sometimes things we treasure most
May be taken away
By things we cannot control,
And we hurt too much to pray.
When, like Job, we're sorely tested
And the agony's severe,
We can cope if we remember
To try and persevere.

If step by step, and day by day
We trust in God above,
He will restore the broken pieces
And fill us with His love.
There are no shortcuts to Heaven,
No pain-free way to go,
But joy comes after the morning
And our faith surely will grow.
Our patience will be rewarded
For faith always conquers fear,
When our resolve is steadfast
And we learn to persevere.

Clay Harrison

A Happy Heart

When I have a happy heart,
All my cares seem to depart;
When on my face I wear a smile,
It lifts my spirits all the while.

When my heart is happy, I...
Feel as free as a butterfly;
When I have hope, then joy is mine
And I can feel God's love divine.

When my heart is happy, all...
The world is at my beck and call,
And a happy heart like a rose bouquet
Is happier when it's given away.

Nora M. Bozeman

A Word Plain and Simple

I've gained true meaning of a word
That I sought through long years of prayer.
It was a word I seldom heard,
Though I knew it was always there.

I sought it in my carnal way,
And for a moment thought I'd be
On top of the world for a day;
But alas! It rejected me.

I found it when I shared my plight
With a dear and most cherished friend.
That word burst forth in shining light,
And my search had come to an end.

What is this one word? I'll tell you.
It is a word that we all need.
The only word in life that's true:
It's "Love" plain and simple, indeed!

Henry W. Gurley

Balance

When work becomes "life,"
Where's time for fun?
There's only enough time
To get more work done!

Where is the time
To pay attention
To loved ones around you
Too numerous to mention?

And God waits for us
To want His direction
In all things we do
With love and affection!

Work is so satisfying
But something is greater;
It's wanting God's Will,
Who is Lord and Creator.

He'll give us the balance
We need each day
To love Him and serve Him
And take time to play!

Margaret Peterson

Lord,

I feel weak and I feel like giving up.
I can't see what else I can do to change
the direction of my life and make it
positive once more. I know that Your power is
made perfect in weakness. I pray for that
incredible power to rest on me and pull me
through these testing times. Shelter me
through this storm and let me feel Your sun
shining down on me once again.

Amen

With You in the Rain

The closest we can feel to God
Is in the depths of pain
To feel His presence in the storm,
His peace within the rain.

To know He loves us as we are
In spite of things we've done,
To know His love cannot be earned
But given by His Son.

How can we not give our best
No matter what life brings;
He gave His all that we might live
And gives us all good things.

So, in the midst of sorrow
Or in the depths of pain,
Remember God, who gave his Son,
Is with you in the rain.

Jill Lemming

*"I would soon find a shelter from the
raging wind and storm."*
Psalm 55:9

23

Godly Zeal

The Christian person should possess,
A deep devotion and Godly zeal.
We each should serve with vigor,
As we strive to do God's Will.

So many sad and hurting people
Are looking for someone to care.
We need to reach out in compassion,
With God's message of love from despair.

We can always offer assistance to them,
Showing we are willing to try…
Meeting the need as best we can,
Without asking when, if or why.

Our Lord commissioned us to serve Him,
And serving others is doing the same...
For what we do unto others,
We should do it in Jesus's Name.

Our life and work should be a prayer –
Dear God, help me serve with zeal.
May I never be too busy or tired
To show my love for You is real.

Frances Culp Wolfe

*But you, man of God, avoid
all this. Instead, pursue
righteousness, devotion, faith,
love, patience, and gentleness.*
1 Timothy 6:11

Seeing the Face of Jesus

Until we can recognize the face of Jesus
In every person that we see,
We haven't found the true love
That God meant for there to be.

When we see the pain and suffering
In our brothers' sorrowful eyes,
We must take the time to comfort them
As we hear their mournful cries.

We must soothe their troubled hearts
Until their sobs have long ceased;
Then feed the poor and hungry
Until their appetites are appeased.

The homeless and less fortunate
Have a soul like you and me.
If we look at them with true faith,
Then it's Jesus's face we'll see.

Shirley Hile Powell

Peace

Sometimes when life seems harsh and dreary,
When demands, needs and qualms make me weary,
I turn to prayer for peace of soul
And rethink my life's aim and ultimate goal.

Thank God for His Word to which I turn
When life brands me and my soul does burn.
Thank God for Jesus, His Son, Who died
So my sins and my failings are atrophied.

The Holy Spirit guides me when I am weak
To turn to God for the peace I seek,
His hand in mine, His arm lovingly given
To help me remember my path to Heaven.

The peace I seek none here can bestow,
The answer is You and Your Word to know.
Thank You for hours, days, months and years
When You have helped me see hope in spite of tears.

Your blessings have showered my every life moment,
Your peace came to me in the midst of torment.
Peace is mine if I just seek You.
Peace is yours – He loves you, too!

Margaret Linfield

Turn from evil and do good;
seek peace and pursue it.
Psalm 34:15

The Order of the Day

Now, if kindness and patience
Are the order of the day,
Then there will be no angry
Or unpleasant things to say.
And if more thought is given
To the other person's needs,
Then there will be more room for
Politeness and courtesy.
And if the heart will follow,
Then the Lord will surely lead…
It to a much better life,
And meaningful days, indeed.

Steven Michael Schumacher

Tears

God gave us tears to be released
When emotions overcome,
And tears do not dry up with age –
They're there for everyone.

Tears help to cleanse our minds and hearts,
And give us great relief,
When we are in the midst of joy
Or in the throes of grief.

So, let the water of your soul
Fall freely down your face;
For tears were given with a purpose,
And they have a time and place.

Sharon Fuqua

*On the day the Lord relieves you of
sorrow and unrest and the hard service
in which you have been enslaved…*
Isaiah 14:3

31

Make known to me Your ways, Lord; teach me Your paths. Guide me in Your truth and teach me, for You are God my Savior. For You I wait all the long day, because of Your goodness, Lord.
Psalm 25:4-5

It's Time to Pray

If remnants of the past come up
And over you hold sway,
It isn't time to sit and cry –
It's only time to pray.

If troubles surge about you,
Looming larger every day,
It isn't time to cover, no –
It's simply time to pray.

It's such a simple answer
And it's free to everyone
Who takes their life more seriously –
For life is more than fun.

It's simply steps to Heaven,
Take Christ's hand and stoutly say,
"I recognize temptation now –
The answer is to pray."

Margaret Peterson

But I pray to You, Lord, for the
time of Your favor. God, in Your
great kindness answer me with
Your constant help.
Psalm 69:14

Forgive and Forget

Fully forgive and fully forget
Those who sinned against you.
We've been forgiven by God's Son,
We must forgive others, too.

On the Cross Jesus suffered
For our guilt and shame.
Sins have all been forgiven –
We must do the same.

Edna Massimilla

So Easy

God works for the good of those who love Him;
Of this much we must be assured.
In suffering, submitting to His Will,
We'll overcome if we've endured...

By placing our pains and persecutions,
An act of our personal will;
No need for any of us to suffer
As we ascend life's steepest hill.

Alone, and in doubt none of us should be,
His crystal message loud and clear.
We know He gives His divine direction,
And foremost to all He is near.

It's easy! Listen to His Word.
It's easy! Commit to the Lord.

Henry W. Gurley

*"For My yoke is easy,
and My burden light."*
Matthew 11:30

Then your light shall break forth like the dawn, and your wound shall quickly be healed; your vindication shall go before you, and the glory of the Lord shall be your rear guard.

Isaiah 58:8

Light Will Break Through

Cold morning mist – oh how it lingers,
Draping the earth in gray obscurity.
It is so still, no breezes whisper,
No birds repeat their joyful melody.

Only wild geese find their way through the heavens,
With rushing wings they part the hovering mist.
I know that before long the fog is lifting,
My little world appears again, sun-kissed.

Like the fog on a November morning,
Subtly concealing earth and sky from view,
So lies the future, veiled from our vision;
But by and by, light will be breaking through.

Regina Wiencek

Sing to God a new song;
skillfully play with joyful chant.
Psalm 33:3

The Universal Language

Language can be a great barrier,
With people diverse and apart;
When we can't witness by speaking,
We have to depend on the heart.

If you see someone who's hurting,
And there is a desire to uplift;
Compassion should be your motive,
With love as the genuine gift.

Words that are put into action
Will put true love to the test;
For only by giving and sharing,
Can we offer others our best.

No matter the need or the culture,
Whether home or across the great sea,
One language that is universal
Is love – and it always will be.

Frances Culp Wolfe

Lord, do not withhold Your
compassion from me; may Your
enduring kindness ever preserve me.
Psalm 40:12

All It Takes Is a Smile

A smile is a happiness gift,
A lost and lonely heart it can lift;
So why not make someone's life worthwhile –
All it takes is a smile.

A smile is a bridge to the heart,
Joy it will bring you right from the start;
Your day will be happier all the while –
All it takes is a smile.

You can give this life-giving gift,
Whenever someone's soul is adrift;
Smiles will never go out of style –
Yes, all it takes is a smile.

Nora M. Bozeman

Do It Today

How often do we say these words
Before we go to bed…
"Tomorrow is another day
In which to get ahead"?
How often do we put aside
Our problems of today
And think that somewhere, somehow
There will be a brighter way?
We try to use a future scale
For every pound and ounce,
And do not realize that today
Is all that really counts.
Tomorrow is a distant time
And it may never be,
As there may come a sudden end
To all of history.
So, let us do the best we can
In every noble way,
And let us try to do it while
Today is still today.

James J. Metcalf

"*Now forgive my sin, and return with me, that I may worship the Lord.*"
1 Samuel 15:25

Casting Stones

Not one of us is perfect –
We're sinners saved by grace,
So why do some keep casting stones
At others who lose face?
"To err is human," it is said;
It isn't hard to do,
For that deer in the headlights
One day could be you!

To fall from grace is painful,
To forgive is divine,
For sorrows can come in bunches
Like grapes upon a vine.
Sometimes life can be painful
With no relief in sight,
When it seems like every hour
Is multiplied at night.

If Christ had not forgiven us,
How sad would be our fate,
For on the cross He took our place –
His blood wiped clean our slate!
Forgiveness is the anodyne
That consecrates the soul
And repairs the broken pieces
That we can be made whole.

Clay Harrison

I know God has a plan.

I pray for direction to follow it,

patience to wait on it,

and knowledge to know

when it comes.

Unknown

Pray Before Planning

Pray before planning
The rest of your day.
Welcome Him in
And hear what He'd say.
Changes may follow
From what you had thought,
But let them flow freely –
It won't be for naught.
Could be a door opens
Far down the hall,
Or maybe you stumble
And maybe you fall;
But the Lord's there to guide you
And show you the way,
So, pray before planning –
Hear what He'd say.

Ruthmarie Brooks Silver

Beyond His Care

We cannot drift beyond His care,
His loving arms are everywhere.
From view our loved ones disappear
But we'll still feel their presence here.

We cannot drift beyond His care,
For who goes first will yet remain
Within God's sweet and safe domain,
Their love for us still be the same.

We cannot drift beyond His care,
Though gone, with love and tenderness,
While waiting 'til we meet them there,
Loved ones are kept and daily blessed.

No, we can't drift beyond His care,
His love surrounds us everywhere,
And though we miss those gone ahead,
Someday, eternity we'll share.

Helen Gleason

Depend

We depend on one another,
No one lives just for oneself.
For our food depends on farmers;
We share knowledge for our health.

We depend on publications
To update us on all news.
We depend on other nations
To compare their thoughts and views.

We need priests, rabbis and pastors;
Depend on each – a spiritual guide.
We need teachers for our children,
We need leaders, far and wide.

We depend on those around us…
A helping hand, a neighbor, friend.
We depend on one another –
And, on our Lord, we all depend.

Edna Massimilla

Sorrows Often Beget Blessings

Sorrows often beget blessings
When all is said and done,
For when the storm is over,
We welcome back the sun.
There will be things that test our faith
And stumbling blocks ahead,
But each time we overcome them,
Our faith is being fed.

The road of life is bumpy
But we can make it through,
For God will send His angels
To watch over you.
There are friends who will uphold you
Beneath the wings of prayer,
And they'll be there to support you
Because they truly care.

The things we take for granted
Can quickly fade away,
So we should praise and thank Him
For what we have today.
We must endure the darkness to
Appreciate the sun.
Sorrows often beget blessings
When all is said and done.

Clay Harrison

*They will receive blessings
from the Lord, and justice
from their saving God.*
Psalm 24:5

We May Not See

We may not see the breeze
When God caresses the trees.
We may not see the beauty of heart
But it's where all wonderful things start.
We may not see God's face
But we can feel His embrace.
We may not see the Holy Trinity
But He's One for eternity.
We may not see the Holy Spirit,
But it fills the air for all who are near it.
We may not see what the future brings
But for those who trust God – such wondrous things.

Chet Stanhope

Hello

It was just a simple "hello"
That brought a smile to her face.
Not some gift of purest gold,
Nor silks or satins edged with lace.

Just look at the possibilities
Awaiting some first hello.
Close friendships could be a bonus
With the folks you get to know.

M. Elaine Fowser

Continue Your kindness toward
Your friends, Your just defense
of the honest heart.
Psalm 36:11

Invitation

"My soul is longing for You, Jesus,
Come into my soul.
My heart is yearning for You, Jesus,
Come into my heart."
Jesus will hear your invitation,
Grant your petition when you ask.
He'll be with you through duration,
Helping you fulfill your task.
Unlock barriers that keep Him away,
Welcome Him with open arms.
Implore the Lord this very day –
He will always keep you from harm.
If you but request His presence,
Peace and calm will prevail.
Heart and soul filled with His essence,
Trust in Him will never fail.

Floriana Hall

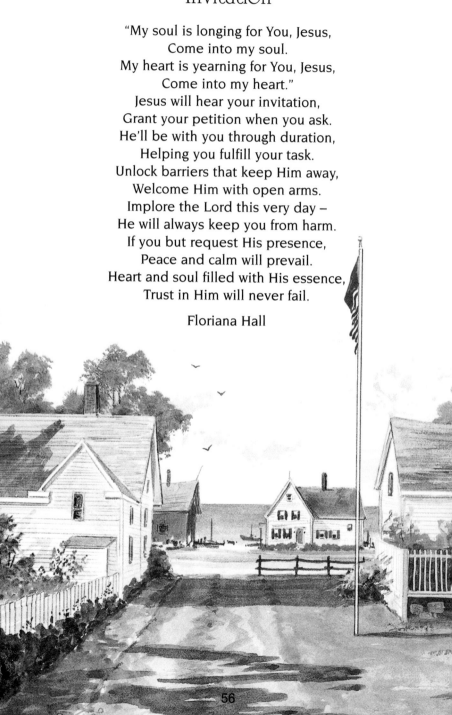

"*If you come with us, we will share with you the prosperity the Lord will bestow on us.*"
Numbers 10:32

How precious to me are
Your designs, O God; how
vast the sum of them!
Psalm 139:17

Only One You

This statement is true! There's only one "you" –
The "you" that God Himself planned!
You are custom-designed, one-of-a-kind,
Shaped by the Master's hand.

Amazing creation, cause for celebration,
This wonderful "you" that God made;
A real work of art, a piece of His heart,
The genius of God on parade.

Let your specialties shine; they are all gifts divine,
Reflecting God's marvelous light.
Only you can be you, unique through and through,
Bringing the Father delight.

So, believe that it's true! There's only one "you" –
The "you" that God Himself planned!
You are custom-designed, one-of-a-kind,
Shaped by the Master's hand.

Idella Pearl Edwards

Majestic and glorious is Your
work, Your wise design
endures forever.
Psalm 111:3

If Only I Had Known

If only I had known
How swiftly time flies,
I would have realized
How quickly things die.

Our time here on earth
Is just a passing through;
Our goal is being in Heaven
Where all things are made new.

If only I had known
That my good deeds on earth
Meant more to my God
Than all of my worth…

I would have shared
More talent and time
With the sad and the lonely
And with all of mankind.

If only I had known
That my Lord would intercede
To grant me His wisdom
And to meet my every need…

I would have known God loves me
For the child that I am;
And when I meet Him in Heaven
I'll be made whole again.

Shirley Hile Powell

Who Am I?

Who am I, that God has made
This beautiful world for me?
He holds the earth in His hands,
Yet is mindful of my needs!

Who am I, that God has paid
The awful price for my sins,
And then chose my very soul
To place His Spirit within?

Steven Michael Schumacher

Problems

Be thankful for problems for they make us pray,
And prayer keeps us close to the Lord.
Without them, we'd spend our time largely on ourselves
Thinking how not to be bored.

But something else happens deep in our soul,
The part that never will die…
Prayer makes us want to draw closer yet,
And sorrow for sin makes us cry.

Tears that are shed in sorrow for sin
Are the best kind of tears in God's eyes.
It shows we appreciate His dear Son's death
Under dark and lonely skies.

We need all our problems – our connection to God.
If you see someone running away,
Tell them they're missing the heart of life
If they don't accept problems and pray.

Margaret Peterson

*And let the peace of Christ
control your hearts, the
peace into which you were
also called in one body.
And be thankful.
Colossians 3:15*

Yesterday and Today

Yesterday, my soul was not to be found –
It was lost in a sea of despair.
To hide the pain, I ran to oblivion,
Nothing on this earth for which to care.

Yesterday, my heart was as cold as a stone,
Nothing could happen to turn it around.
So often hurt in the life of its past,
It seemed buried in the dark, damp ground.

Then, one day, a miracle did free my soul –
My heart began to beat anew;
Despair was replaced with joy and grace,
The pain, now gone, floated aloft and flew.

Today, I can see the road that was taken
Was the path needed to walk, to know
The grace of my Father from up on high –
The real freedom that allows me to grow.

Randi Cook

Lord,

For every opportunity
to walk in Your light,
and to change a life –
I thank You.
For all the different ways
You renew my faith,
never giving up on me –
I thank You.
For every reminder that
I am unique,
here for a reason –
I thank You.
For uplifting me through
the joy of gratitude
and connection,
I thank You, Lord,
now and forever.

Amen

Life's Sunrises and Sunsets

Have you ever watched the sunrise
As it rises in the eastern sky,
How it slowly leaves the horizon
And a new day dawns on high?

Have you ever been amazed by its beauty
When the sun sets in the western sky,
How it leaves behind an array of color
And recedes from its watchful eye?

Now darkness is soon to follow,
'Tis the final hours of the day;
When compared to the span of our lifetime,
We'll liken our days this way.

So we must live each day to the fullest,
And to God be faithful and true,
From the time of our life's sunrise
Until life's sunset is due.

Hazel Yoho

*And now may the Lord be kind and
faithful to you. I, too, will be generous
to you for having done this.*
2 Samuel 2:6

Who Cares?

When you feel that God's not near
And life has gone astray,
Stop and look around you,
And don't just "think," but pray.
It's very hard when you've lost hope
To get down on your knees.
Your life's in desperation,
And there's nothing that will please.
But discipline's required
To use in any way;
Even through that side of doubt,
Get on your knees and pray.

It may take minutes, hours or days,
It may take months or years;
But all the prayers you've shared with Him
Will not fall on deaf ears.
He loves you in each thought and deed
In everything you do;
And one day 'fore you know it,
The sun will shine right through!

Ruthmarie Brooks Silver

...established forever and ever, to
be observed with loyalty and care.
Psalm 111:8

From My Window

From my window I can see
My neighbor's puppies romping free.
God shares His gifts in unexpected ways,
Like when I watch these puppies play.
They make me smile, and break up the day,
These little ones just seem to say…
"Come join the fun, come pet me, please,
You'll feel much better in the open breeze!"
From my window I can see
It's enough to know my spirit's free.

Barbara Joan Million

*Instead, I hope to see you soon,
when we can talk face to face.*
3 John 1:14

71

Jewels

So many gems from which to choose!
We search for one with perfect light,
The fire, the very essence of
A bauble… rare with facets bright.
Its brilliance wakens memories
From snug repose, or restless sleep;
Arousing embers into flame,
As we cull through the sparkling heap.
Words! These are jewels! Sculptor's tool,
That shape our thoughts, in book or score;
Read, sung, recited… memorized,
They flash, like jewels, from heart's store.

Anna Lee Edwards McAlpin

"If, then, you truly heed My commandments which I enjoin on you today, loving and serving the Lord, your God, with all your heart and all your soul..."
Deuteronomy 11:13

It Takes an Effort

It takes an effort to go to church,
When Saturday's chores aren't done,
And it takes an effort to run the race,
Until it is finally won.

It takes an effort to rise in the morn,
When the blankets are snuggly warm,
And it takes an effort to raise a child,
From the very day he is born.

Life's full of efforts, it's certainly true,
And the very least you can do
Is to choose to live for the very One,
Who put forth an effort for you.

Connie J. Kirby

*For this very reason, make every
effort to supplement your faith with
virtue, virtue with knowledge.*
2 Peter 1:5

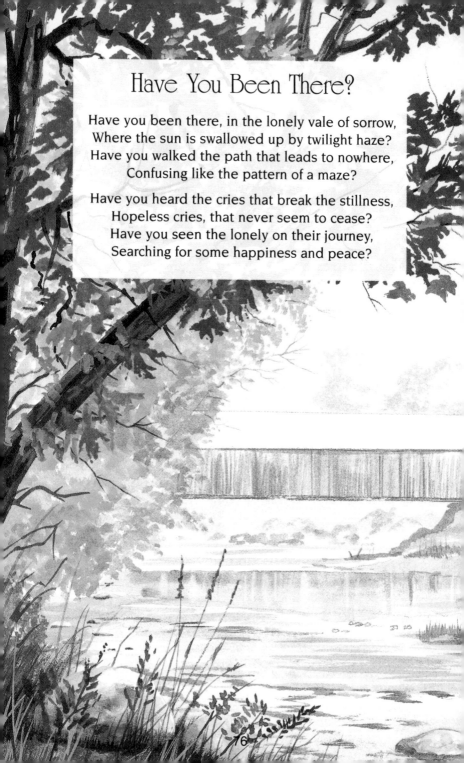

Have You Been There?

Have you been there, in the lonely vale of sorrow,
Where the sun is swallowed up by twilight haze?
Have you walked the path that leads to nowhere,
Confusing like the pattern of a maze?

Have you heard the cries that break the stillness,
Hopeless cries, that never seem to cease?
Have you seen the lonely on their journey,
Searching for some happiness and peace?

Have you seen the eyes that lost their sparkle
In faces deeply etched by sorrow's touch?
Have you given them a word of comfort,
Extending friendship, which they need so much?

Have you given of your time and talents
To a wounded heart, that quivers like a sheaf?
Have you sought the ones left sorrow-stricken
Entering their lonely world of grief?

To the hurting, be God's hand extended,
In a troubled world so filled with hate and woe,
Freely giving of yourself to others;
As you have received, so let love flow.

Regina Wiencek

Joy

If joy could be bought at a local store,
Oh, what a long line there'd be
For people to purchase as much as they could,
Hoping it would last endlessly.

There actually is an endless supply
But it's caused by each one's decision
To give control of their life to the Lord
In penitent, loving submission.

In giving we find that the Bible speaks truth;
It's there for all to believe.
We must lose our life to find it in Christ,
Who is joy and will never deceive.

Margaret Peterson

Unforgotten Song

I care for you in many ways –
I always have, you know.
I take your memory in my heart
Everywhere I go.
Because of you the world becomes
A better place to live,
And I am blessed in every way
By all the love you give.

By your own example
I have learned to put aside
Impatience, doubt and anger,
And to take life in my stride.
You know the song within my heart,
And when the light grows dim,
You sing to me the words long after…
I've forgotten them.

Grace E. Easley

Dear God,

Lift me up for
Your blessings today.
I pray You will anoint me
with strength and self-care.
Grace me with patience
and wisdom. Fill me
with serenity.
Amen

Do good, Lord, to the good, to those who are upright of heart.
Psalm 125:4

People Are Good at Heart

Despite everything, I believe
That people are good at heart,
Because the Lord God made us all,
And gave each of us a part
To serve in His great plan of love,
And no one's part is too small –
By serving others, we answer
Our dear Savior's holy call.
Everyone has imperfections,
But putting such things aside,
The goodness of God in people
Keeps our hope in life alive.

Steven Michael Schumacher

He Hears Us

Did you ever wake up in the morning
Wondering what today will unfold;
Will it be bright and sunny
With colors and hues so bold?
Or will the day be cloudy
With waves billowing to and fro –
Damp and dark and chilly
With winds that fiercely blow?
Through the sunshine and the shadows
God hears our humblest cry;
He knows when our hearts grow weary
Or when we're wondering why.

For life isn't always rosebuds
And cheery, sun-filled days –
Ofttimes it's blizzards and snow storms
And shades of black and gray.
Yet God will never forsake us
And He knows sometimes we're frail;
It's on bended knees we're strongest –
So cry out, He'll hear your troubled tale!
Oh, lift your heart towards Heaven
And believe as you praise and sing,
For God's phone line is never too busy,
And He hears the faintest ring-a-ling.

Linda C. Grazulis

Light is sweet! And it is pleasant for the eyes to see the sun.
Ecclesiastes 11:7

How Fair the Day!

Think pleasant thoughts and you will see
How much better off you'll be…
Let them begin as you awake;
Look out and watch the morning break.
Night has driven the storm clouds away
And oh, how fair, how fair the day!

Think kind thoughts, like something you could do
For someone who is less fortunate than you…
Now, that's a very pleasant thought, indeed,
To help someone who is in need.
Or write to a lonely one far away,
Then, they too shall see how fair the day!

Think happy thoughts, watch children at play,
Running barefoot on a warm Summer day…
Hear their laughter, hear them sing,
Making life seem a magical thing…
And with the sun beaming down its brightest ray,
Oh, how fair, how fair the day!

Lou Ella Cullipher

*Her ways are pleasant
ways, and all her
paths are peace.*
Proverbs 3:17

The Things That Last Forever

The things that last forever
Aren't found in any store.
They are the things eternal
God blesses evermore.
There are temporary pleasures
Derived from store-bought things,
But they cannot hold a candle
To the joy salvation brings!

The things that last forever
Are stored within the heart,
The simple acts of kindness
That set our lives apart.
To know someone cares enough
To pray for you each day
Keeps tugging at your heartstrings
As the years fade away.

When we put faith into action,
It's amazing how it grows,
And when your heart is filled with love,
It's amazing how it shows!
The world and all its treasures
Can't unlock Heaven's door.
The things that last forever
Aren't found in any store.

Clay Harrison

The Lord shall reign
forever and ever.
Exodus 15:18

Rough Roads

How many rough roads have you traveled
Thinking you had lost your way?
But when life's roads bring us to our knees,
It is there we learn to pray.

In times like these, God has His reasons
To increase our faith in Him.
Too many times, when the way is easy,
We drift with the crowd into sin.

So, thank You, Lord, for the trials
You see fit to send our way,
To keep our focus on the One
Who is our Guide day after day.

M. Elaine Fowser

Ways to Thank Almighty God

There are many ways to thank Almighty God:

Observing the sunrise in full view,
Storing memories of each spectacular hue;

Feeling the crisp morning wind upon my cheeks,
Listening to the whip-poor-will when he speaks.

Thanks can be a still prayerful heart,
The smile on my face as the long day departs;

Peace in the soul as day turns to night,
Wonder about the stars shining bright.

It's easy to have a heart filled with prayer,
For God and His blessings are everywhere.

Barbara Joan Million

For the spirit of God has
made me, the breath of the
Almighty keeps me alive.
Job 33:4

When Troubles Bring You to Your Knees

When troubles bring you to your knees,
Pause and say a prayer.
Your burdens will feel lighter,
For God will meet you there.
When you're feeling disconnected,
Set apart from the crowd,
It's no time for being stubborn,
No time for being proud.

When you're standing at life's crossroads,
Don't know which way to go,
It's time to set priorities
While pacing to and fro.
God has a plan for every life
And He will lead the way,
If only we will talk to Him
And take the time to pray.

There are things we cannot change,
Things beyond our control,
But God always gives directions
In matters of the soul.
When the life you build is broken,
In need of much repair,
And troubles bring you to your knees –
Pause and say a prayer.

Clay Harrison

My Faith

My faith is grounded and unshakable
No matter where I kneel;
My faith is that familiar fence
Though blinded I can feel.
My faith is like the breaking sun
Through gloomiest of days;
A ray of light to pierce the storm
That I may find my way.
My faith cannot be swept away
By current strong or deep,
For it is anchored in the truth
Of evidence not seen.
My faith is not a flower
Slowly wilting in the dark,
No, rather ever blossoming
With light eternal in my heart.

Jodie Hoover

Just Ask

Do you ever wonder why we fail
At things we try to do,
Or why we seldom find the peace
In trials that we go through?
So many times we haven't stopped
To ask the Lord's advice…
To open up our hearts to Him,
Or offer up our lives.
We make it harder on ourselves
When we face trials as one,
For all we really need to do
Is trust our Father's Son.
Hand your burdens over now
And give your heart a rest –
Jesus knows your every need,
His way is for the best.
All your troubles, all your trials
Are safe within His grasp –
Nothing is too great for Him,
If all you'll do is ask.

Jill Lemming

Any Day and Every Day

Any day and every day
Can be a special one,
Filled with joy and happiness,
Encouragement and fun.
The main ingredient life needs
To transform days for you
Is having Jesus in your heart –
Each day He'll see you through.
He'll hold your hand and guide your step,
He'll love you to the end.
Nothing else can brighten days
Like Jesus as your Friend.

Bonnie L. Nelson

The thoughtful man will not neglect
direction; the proud and insolent
man is deterred by nothing.
Sirach 32:18

Two Footprints

I know this is a time of confusion and strife,
Not knowing the direction to take in life.
Seemingly dark wherever you turn
And not rewarded for showing concern.

Your efforts you feel always worked somehow –
At night you awake and wonder why not now?
Because life moves on to a different phase,
It's time for a change to brighter days.

The tunnel's so dark, at the end a wee light;
Hold fast to a plan until it gets bright.
"Have faith, My son, take time to pray,
Believe in Me," the Lord would say.

A trial, perhaps to see if we hold,
To wait on God for what will unfold.
Each day's a beginning of new things ahead,
We must die to self before we are led.

I struggle, too, with these things that I write,
I've crawled through tunnels to reach that light.
I don't want to let go, as He holds my hand,
Many times I've looked back at two footprints in the sand.

Vivian Faught

*But I believe I shall enjoy the Lord's
goodness in the land of the living.*
Psalm 27:13

His Presence Within

Far above the bustling crowds,
Beyond blue skies and fluffy clouds,
High above the sun's golden rays,
The night's faint light and milky way,
Enthroned in His heavenly heights,
God is surrounded by glorious light.
And though we seem so far apart,
When we seek Him in our hearts,
Quietly in His gentle way,
He speaks to us in many ways,
Not with words we hear out loud;
He does not shout above the crowd,
His presence is felt within –
All praise and glory belong to Him.

Jacqui Richardson

101

Praise Him

Rejoice! Your God is King;
Raise your voices and sing.
Lift up your hearts and adore,
Your God reigns forevermore.

Rejoice! Your God is Lord;
He commands all by His Word.
He's Lord of sun, moon and stars,
He's sufficient for every cause.

By His creative hand,
He made mountains, oceans, land.
He made us, too – you and I,
To lift His Name up on high.

So, to our God, let's raise
A paean of joy and praise.
Him only must we adore,
Our God – He reigns forevermore!

Nellie Neil

Jesus Understands

Why are we so misunderstood,
As we journey on our way?
It seems that so many find fault
In nearly everything we say…

Why… when you try to do a good deed,
And think everything is well in hand,
Someone will come along
And just won't understand…

The good you tried to do was wrong,
The things you tried to say…
You soon find out that someone
Is misunderstood each day.

But there's one relief in knowing,
Though you may be woman or man,
When all the world misunderstands you,
Jesus understands.

Gloria Garrion

Our Lives

How can we live without sunshine?
How can we live without rain?
How can we live without doctors and nurses
To help relieve our pain?

How can we live without beauty,
The rainbow after the showers,
The warm, rosy sunset and butterflies,
And colorful, fragrant flowers?

But how can we live without Jesus,
Who is always willing to bear
All the worries, troubles and problems
That we like to put in His care?

He is the only true Savior
And we should always worship Him.
With wide-open arms, He will pardon us
And cleanse us from all sin.

Esther Edwards

Give Me Just One Thing Today

This morning I woke up
To a lovely sunny day,
And I began to think of God,
So I began to pray.

"Lord, give me just one thing today
That I can praise You for;
Give me joys to shout about,
A hope for what's in store.

Lord, give me just one thing today
Is all I want to ask,
So I can praise Your Holy Name,
As I go about my tasks."

Although my prayer
Was short in length,
He answered it –
He gave me strength.

Bonnie L. Nelson

Revelation

Now I see but dimly;
Yet one day, face-to-face,
I shall see all things clearly
Through God my Father's grace.
All questions will be answered,
Those mysteries long concealed,
All the hidden things of God
At last will be revealed.
Oh, how I shall rejoice then
To be known as I am known,
To put away my childish ways
And finally be full-grown.

I long for all to be complete,
No longer just a part,
To feel God's great and endless love
Perfected in my heart.
For though I live in faith and hope
Until my life shall cease,
The love He puts within my heart
Is far greater than these.

Marilyn Oakvik

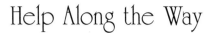

Help Along the Way

I cannot make the sunshine
When the clouds are filled with rain;
I can only share your sorrow
But I cannot ease the pain.

I can give you my shoulder to lean on
When everything seems blue;
I can put my arms around you
And try to help you through.

It's times like these when there's trouble
That you really need a friend;
I'll always be there beside you
And help you 'til you mend.

I can give you all the support you need,
A smile or two along the way;
I can try to give you some happiness
When your skies have turned to gray.

If you learn to laugh as you trod life's paths,
Then walk along with me;
These things I gladly give – for free,
Because once they were given to me.

Lee Rix

An Earnest Plea

You hear every word that is spoken in secret,
You know every thought hidden deeply within.
Oh Lord, direct my wandering footsteps,
Keep me from straying and guard me from sin.
With each dawning day new trials I encounter.
Heartaches are many and tears often flow;
But with each faltering footstep I am taking,
You're walking beside me, peace to bestow.

Help me to remember when shadows are falling,
When all hope lies crushed, You are still by my side.
Never, no, never will You leave, nor forsake me;
Under Your wings I will safely abide.

Regina Wiencek

The Lord has heard my prayer;
the Lord takes up my plea.
Psalm 6:10

It gleamed with the splendor of God.
Its radiance was like that of a precious
stone, like jasper, clear as crystal.
Revelation 21:11

Those Precious In-Betweens

Folks are always in a rush,
Afraid their dreams will gather dust.
But if they'd just slow down a bit
They'd prevent a lot of hit and miss.
"Quickest" is not always best;
There's times when "slow" should be your quest.
Life is short enough, you see…
So fill it to capacity.
Take the time to understand
That "speed" can stop the best laid plans.
If you should stumble on the way,
Begin again without delay;
But don't proceed at break-neck speed
Or you just might miss what's in-between.

Jeanne Paolucci Dunaway

*How precious is Your love, O God! We
take refuge in the shadow of Your wings.*
Psalm 36:8

River of Peace

A river of peace
Flows through my soul,
Renewing my faith
And making me whole.

It's not a still pool
Stagnant and cold,
But a bubbling stream,
Effervescent and bold.

Constantly flowing,
A current so strong;
God's love within me
All my life long.

When I am surrounded
By earthly discord,
I look inward to find
The peace of the Lord.

Micheline Hull Dolan

Praise

Did you ever get up and have a spiraling day
When nothing seemed to go your way,
And you said, "Dear Lord, would You come to me?"
You gazed up at the green-leafed tree,
And on the bird house, a tiny wren
Trilled her song again and again.
Purple petunias adorned the ground,
Yet, peace was nowhere to be found.
Then you said, "Dear Lord, would You come to me?"
And you got down on an aching knee.
You folded your hands, and bowed your head,
When quietly a soft voice said,
"I've come to you in every leaf,
All I need is your belief.
In every flower… in every bird…
The song of Heaven can be heard."

Hazel Sharp

In the Hymn of Prayer

In the hymn of prayer our burdens lay still,
Freeing us from worry, calling us to kneel;
Each moment releases our anguish and sorrow
Made bearably light to face each new tomorrow.

Our bemused and heavy hearts are lifted above
To be blessed and healed by God's wondrous love;
Our torment and grief becomes lost in life's hymn,
While messages of hope release us from sin.

Then, all of our burdens, sorrows and fears
Suddenly flow through heartaches and tears
As God embraces us with pride and such glory –
In the hymn of our prayers we share our life story.

When we lay down our troubles and give Him our all,
Life becomes bearable, problems become small;
The song in our hearts then call Him at will –
In the hymn of our prayers our burdens lay still.

Dianne Cogar

*As they returned, they were
singing hymns and
glorifying Heaven, "for He
is good, for His mercy
endures forever."*
1 Maccabees 4:24

The Greatest Wonder

I'm touched by the greatest wonder on earth
And it came from Heaven above
To dwell in the heart, soul and mind –
The name of it is love.

Love is the peace that overflows
And the joy in a brand-new day.
It's the arms that enfold a crying child
Or the found path when gone astray.

Love can come like a lightning bolt…
A shot right out of the blue.
But when it hits, and it surely will,
It makes our dreams come true.

This is what makes a house a home,
Filled with willingness to forgive.
Being kind to all who enter
Puts the bloom in the life we live.

Love is found o'er all the earth,
Even in the call of a dove.
It is God's gift to you and me;
For God, Himself, is love.

M. Elaine Fowser

*C*reator God, I thank You for everything
You've given me. Everywhere I look, I see
Your creation and I see Your beauty.
In others, I see Your image. At home, I see
the blessings You've given me. In Nature,
I see Your artwork. In the house of the Lord,
I see evidence of repentance,
forgiveness, love, and lives changed.
Thank You for the beauty all around me.

Amen

He's in the Blessings

Look for the blessings every day
And find the Father's heart;
Look for the good things of this world
That His goodness will impart.

Look for His mercy, look for His love,
You'll find it in your midst;
Look for the blessings, if you will,
For that's where the Father is.

Look for the children as they play,
Look at the clear blue sky;
Look at the flowers and the trees,
His creations by and by.

Look for the blessings in your life,
And all that God has done;
Give thanks to the Father every day,
For He is the Holy One.

Jill Lemming

He answered Him, "If I find favor with You, give me a sign that You are speaking with me.
Judges 6:17

When I Was Lost

I've struggled and suffered
Trying to find my own way,
And I've stumbled and fallen
Throughout each day.

I've picked myself up
To dust myself off,
And I've realized that
I've long been lost.

A tear escapes
The corner of my eye.
I fall to my knees
And I look to the sky.

I cry out and pray,
It seems to no avail.
Then, I remember
His compassion never fails.

He has been there for me
Throughout each day,
And His angels have been there
To keep me safe.

Bradley E. Fowler

The Threshing Floor

I seek the peace of God today,
My spirit longs to soar.
It's hard to mount with eagle's wings
Upon this threshing floor.

And though His purpose I can't see,
For shadows dim the glass,
He whispers softly to my heart
That this trial, too, shall pass.

And when I'm feeling tossed about
And battered by the rain,
The Spirit blows the chaff away
To separate the grain.

So, in the midst of burdens great,
My soul does find His peace.
And praying through, His grace sweeps down
To bring me sweet release.

So, I'll defeat this enemy,
For God's strength does not tire.
Then, I will stand as strong and true
As gold tried in the fire.

Robin Gray

God's Presence

God's presence is not in Heaven
Waiting for us to come;
It is with us constantly
As is the daily sun.

From early in the morning
With its glorious light,
Until day is over and we
Settle down at night.

Sometimes we cannot feel it
Or do not take the time,
But it is with us always
In your life and in mine.

Henry Thomas Watkinson